	DATE DUE		

CITIES OF THE WORLD

BUENOS AIRES

BY DEBORAH KENT

CHILDREN'S PRESS®
A Division of Grolier Publishing
New York London Hong Kong Sydney
Danbury, Connecticut

CONSULTANTS

Horacio A. Lombardi, Professor Superior
Instituto Nacional Superior del Profesorado Técnico, Buenos Aires

Linda Cornwell
Learning Resource Consultant
Indiana Department of Education

Project Editor: Downing Publishing Services
Design Director: Karen Kohn & Associates, Ltd.
Photo Researcher: Jan Izzo

NOTES ON SPANISH PRONUNCIATION
Most of the pronunciations in this book are exactly as they look, with the following notes: *ah* is like *a* in father; *ar* and *are* are like *ar* in far; *oh, oe,* and *oa* are like *o* in hope; *oo* is as in food; *igh* is as in light; *oce* is like *os* in post; *ace* is as in race; *zh* is like the *s* in pleasure. Some sounds in Spanish do not occur in English: <u>h</u> is like *h* as in hat, but stronger and harsher. If you try to say *k* as in kite but relax and slur the sound, it will sound like <u>h</u>.

Visit Children's Press on the Internet at:
    http://publishing.grolier.com

Library of Congress Cataloging-in-Publication Data
Kent, Deborah.
        Buenos Aires / by Deborah Kent.
            p. cm — (Cities of the world)
        Includes bibliographical references and index.
        Summary: Describes the history, culture, daily life, food, people, sports, and
    points of interest in the capital and largest city of Argentina, South America, a
    port city on the Río de la Plata.
        ISBN 0-516-20592-7 (lib. bdg.)   0-516-26326-9 (pbk.)
        1. Buenos Aires (Argentina)—Juvenile literature. [1. Buenos Aires (Argentina)]
    I. Title.   II. Series: Cities of the world (New York, N.Y.)
    F3001.K46   1998   97-49507
    982'.11—dc21   CIP
                                                                     AC

TABLE OF CONTENTS

Every Thursday afternoon, a band of women gathers in the Plaza de Mayo in Buenos Aires. The women wear dark, somber clothing. Their faces are marked with anger and sadness. In a determined line, they march around the pyramid that stands at the plaza's center.

Plaza de Mayo (PLAH-sah deh MAH-zhoa)

5

The Mothers of May, as these women call themselves, are mourning sons and daughters lost between 1975 and 1982 in Argentina's "Dirty War." Through those terrible years, an oppressive military dictatorship imprisoned some 10,000 people as enemies of the state. Few of the prisoners were ever heard from again. They simply disappeared. Their mothers and grandmothers have not forgotten the *desaparecidos*, or "disappeared ones." In the Plaza de Mayo, the mothers call the government to account. They grieve and they plead for answers.

The Plaza de Mayo is a broad, grassy square in downtown Buenos Aires. It has witnessed some of the most stirring moments in Argentina's history. In 1810, crowds gathered here to proclaim independence from the ruling Spanish viceroy. In the late 1940s, people packed the plaza to cheer the popular president Juan Perón and his wife Evita. The Peróns often addressed the nation from the balcony of the Presidential Palace. Known as the Casa Rosada (Pink House), the palace stands at the eastern edge of the square.

desaparecidos (DAY-SAH-PAH-REH-SEE-DOCE)

The Mothers of May stage weekly rallies in the Plaza de Mayo demanding information about the fate of the desaparecidos, *their relatives who disappeared during Argentina's "Dirty War."*

By tradition, the Plaza de Mayo is a meeting place. Sometimes, people come here for political rallies. Sometimes, they gather to protest injustice. Most often, they simply meet to enjoy lively conversation. Talking is a favorite Buenos Aires pastime.

During the grim days of the Dirty War, the voices of the Argentine people were hushed by fear. But in 1983, the military dictatorship finally collapsed. Argentina established a democratic government at last. In the years that followed, the people of Buenos Aires tried to put the past behind them as they built new lives. At the Plaza de Mayo, in the heart of their city, they are free once more to speak their minds.

Traditional San Martín Guards (right) stand at attention outside the Presidential Palace (above), which is known as the Casa Rosada.

Juan Perón (HWAHN peh-RONE)
Evita (AY-VEE-TAH)
Casa Rosada (CAH-SAH roe-SAH-DAH)

The vast land of Argentina sprawls across the southern portion of South America. It embraces grassy plains, rugged mountains, and rain forests teeming with wildlife. The capital, Buenos Aires, is by far the nation's largest city. About one of every three Argentines lives in Buenos Aires or its metropolitan area. Argentine poet Martinez Estrada once described Buenos Aires as the "head of Goliath." It is the nerve center of this vast country, like the enormous head of the biblical giant. Whatever happens in Buenos Aires sends ripples throughout the nation.

Martinez Estrada (MAR-TEE-NACE ESS-TRAH-DAH)

THE PORTEÑOS AND THEIR CITY

Buenos Aires lies on the eastern bank of the Río de la Plata, a Spanish name meaning "River of Silver." Actually, the Río de la Plata is not a true river at all. It is an estuary, a long arm of the sea. Buenos Aires does not possess a natural harbor. Yet it is one of the busiest ports in the world. During the nineteenth century, an army of workers dredged a section of the estuary until it was deep enough to berth large cargo ships. The ships carried Argentine goods to Europe. In return, they brought tens

Left: Argentine children
Below: Ships in the Río de la Plata, one of the busiest ports in the world

of thousands of European immigrants to Buenos Aires. Because so many of their ancestors arrived by water, native-born citizens of Buenos Aires call themselves *porteños*, or "people of the port."

If you walk down the street in Buenos Aires you will hear Spanish spoken all around you. Buenos Aires was founded by people from Spain. Spanish is the official language, and a large number of its citizens are of Spanish descent. But the city has also seen heavy immigration from Italy. In the local phone book, Italian names such as Martinelli and Capello outnumber Gómez, Rivera, and other Spanish surnames. Many Buenos Aires restaurants specialize in pasta dishes popular in Naples and Rome. Chefs boast that the noodles are "just like my mama used to make them."

These college students may be porteños, *or native-born Buenos Aires residents.*

Río de la Plata (REE-OH DEH LAH PLAH-TAH) *porteño* (PORE-TANE-YOH)

The sidewalk cafés in Buenos Aires give the city a French flavor. Some restaurants serve English high tea, though they might serve the tea in distinctive Argentinian cups such as the one pictured below.

Immigration from France was never extensive, but Buenos Aires has a strong French flavor. The broad downtown streets look like the tree-lined boulevards of Paris. Well-to-do porteños stroll the pavements in the latest Parisian fashions. Cappuccino and dainty pastries are served in French-style sidewalk cafes. Immigrants from England and Germany have also left their stamp on Buenos Aires. Some restaurants serve English high tea, a light afternoon meal of sandwiches, cakes, and tea. Others feature German beer and sausage. On first glance, Buenos Aires appears to be a thoroughly European city. According to a popular saying, a porteño is an Italian who speaks Spanish, thinks of himself as an Englishman, and behaves as if he were French.

Flowering trees in Plaza San Martín

As you cross a Buenos Aires park, you will see palm trees, jacarandas, and bougainvilleas with purple flowers. Here and there, a hummingbird flashes like a tiny jewel. Buenos Aires lies well south of the equator. Children begin summer vacation in December and return to school early in March. Though most porteños are of European stock, their city is South American at heart.

A CITY OF OUTSIDERS

In 1992, a gleaming shopping mall opened in downtown Buenos Aires. Its soaring dome is painted with murals by Argentina's finest artists. The mall occupies the site of the old Pacific Railroad Station. For generations, trains brought people to the capital from far-flung villages all across the country. Like the immigrants from overseas, they came in hope of finding work and building a better life.

Jammed into rattling automobiles, packed onto crowded buses amid bags and boxes, villagers still stream into Buenos Aires. They come to escape the relentless poverty of the back country. Like those before them, they are drawn by the promise of work and the excitement of the capital. Established porteños tend to look down on these newcomers, referring to them as "outsiders." Like other immigrants, the "outsiders" carve out a place for themselves and make the city their home.

This Buenos Aires artisan is making decorative items from straw.

Not all of the "outsiders" are Argentines. Today, most of them come over the borders from Paraguay, Bolivia, Uruguay, and Brazil. Other recent immigrants are from Korea, Armenia, Lebanon, and Syria. Their cuisines, languages, and customs give the city a diversity it never knew before.

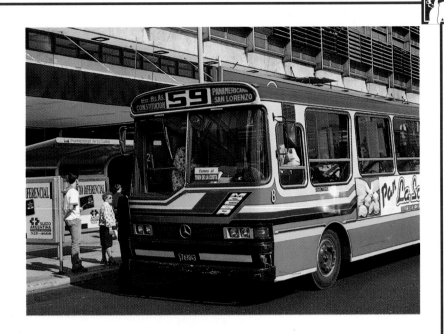

A public bus picks up passengers on the Avenida Nueve de Julio.

This gleaming new shopping mall, the Galerías Pacífico, was built in the old Pacific Railroad Station.

Jobs are scarce for the newcomers, and the pay is pitifully low. Most new arrivals settle in noisy, densely crowded slums known as *villas miserias*. Many of these neighborhoods do not even have names. Instead, the government assigns them numbers: Villa 7, Villa 14, Villa 24. The dirt streets of the villa miseria are dusty in dry weather and turn to mud when it rains.

Flooding is a serious problem. In some neighborhoods, people fill buckets at public taps on the street because their homes lack running water.

In some ways, the newcomers have simply traded one form of poverty for another. Yet few choose to return to their villages. As long as they stay in Buenos Aires, they can always take a city bus downtown. They can gaze into shop windows, study movie marquees, and watch rich passersby in Parisian clothes. If fortune is kind, perhaps one day the girl from Villa 7 will wear a suit and work in a downtown office. Perhaps some day the boy from Villa 24 will rent a fancy apartment high above the wide, bustling streets. Perhaps. Perhaps.

villa miseria
(VEE-ZHAH MEE-SAY-REE-AH)
Carlos Saúl Menem
(CAR-LOCE SAH-OOL MEH-NEMM)

The Obelisk, which was built to mark the 400th anniversary of the founding of Buenos Aires, occupies a place of honor on the Avenida Nueve de Julio.

The Peddler's Son in the Pink House

In 1989, the people of Argentina elected Carlos Saúl Menem to serve as their president. Menem was the son of Muslim Syrian immigrants. His father was a street peddler. Menem became the first Muslim to occupy the Pink House, or Presidential Palace.

1991
InterAmerican
Petroleum
& Gas
Conference

IPGC

Houston, Texas
November 13-15, 1991

THE CITY THAT NEVER SLEEPS

Porteños and newcomers love to go to the movies. Lavalle Street in downtown Buenos Aires is lined with cinemas that show a wide array of Argentine and foreign films. On the weekends, people line up for the last show, which begins at midnight. When the show lets out two hours later, the moviegoers are still wide awake and ready for more fun. They flock to cafés and pizzerías for a late supper—or is it a very early breakfast? Then they move on to their favorite nightclubs for music and dancing. Finally, at dawn, they stumble home to bed.

During the day, the downtown streets throng with office workers and shoppers. Two major streets, Lavalle and Florida, are pedestrian shopping malls. The city's most expensive stores are found along Alvear, Quintana, and Santa Fe Avenues. If you want a fine leather vest, a fur cape, or a diamond ring, this is the place to go. Even if your wallet is empty, you can join the crowds of window-shoppers.

Except for the pedestrian malls, Buenos Aires is clogged with traffic day and night. Many of the vehicles on the streets are brightly colored buses called *colectivos*.

Even those people who have no money in their coin purses can enjoy a wonderful window-shopping experience in Buenos Aires.

Young women shopping on Calle Florida, a pedestrian shopping mall

Beautiful painted-tile artwork decorates some of the city's subway stations.

The colectivos are the city's chief means of public transportation. Buenos Aires also has a subway system with 23 miles (37 kilometers) of track, which was built in 1912.

Buenos Aires is a very modern city. But here and there amid the high-rise buildings and traffic islands you can still glance back into the city's past.

Lavalle (LAH-VAH-zeh)
Florida (FLOE-REE-dah)
Alvear (AHL-vay-ARE)
Quintana (KEEN-TAH-nah)
Santa Fe (SAHN-tah FAY)
colectivo (COH-LECK-TEE-voh)

GOOD AIR

Lezama Park is a popular picnic spot for Buenos Aires families. Few pause to remember that in 1536, a band of Spaniards under Captain Pedro de Mendoza tried to build a settlement near this site. Within a few years, the original inhabitants, the Querandí Indians, drove the Europeans away. But in 1580, another Spaniard, Juan de Garay, brought a fresh group of settlers. They named the place for their patron saint, Nuestra Senora de los Buenos Aires, Our Lady of the Good Air. This time, the Spaniards had come to stay.

Lezama (LEH-SAH-MAH)
Pedro de Mendoza (PEH-DROH DEH MEN-DOE-
 SAH)
Querandí (KEH-RAHN-DEE)
Juan de Garay (HWAHN DEH GAH-RYE)
Nuestra Senora de los Buenos Aires
 (NWACE-TRAH SENN-YORE-AH DEH LOCE BWAY-
  NOCE EYE-RACE)

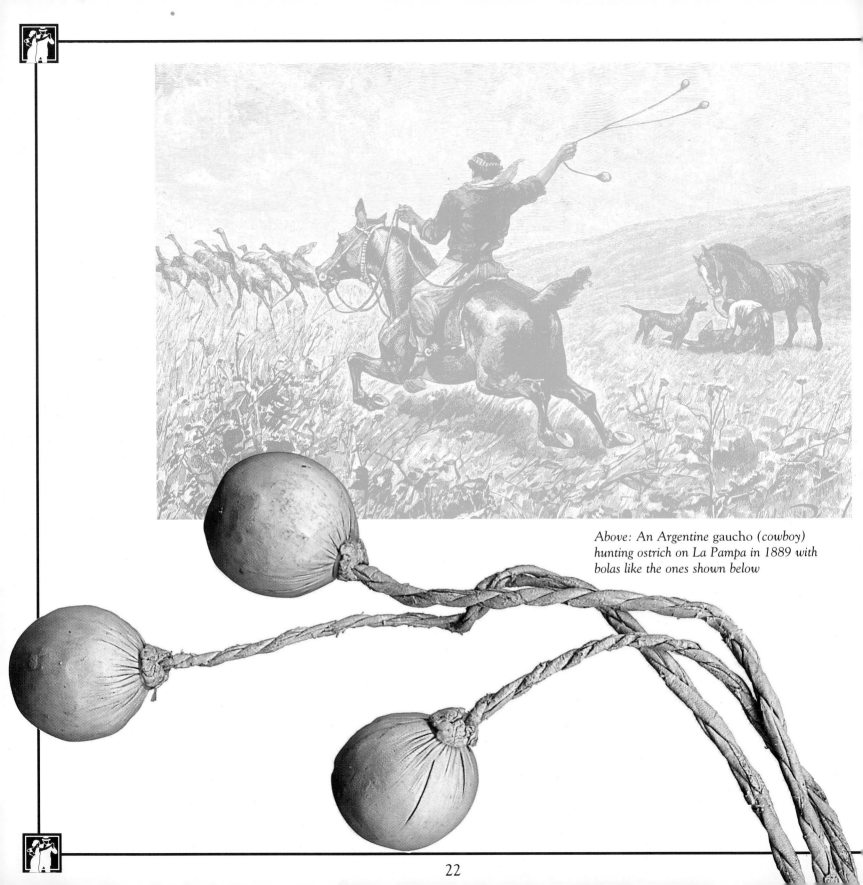

Above: An Argentine gaucho (cowboy)
hunting ostrich on La Pampa in 1889 with
bolas like the ones shown below

THE FORGOTTEN OUTPOST

During the 1500s, Spain was the most powerful nation on earth. Its vast empire included all of Latin America with the exception of Brazil. In South America, Spanish power centered in Lima, Peru, on the Pacific coast. Spain hardly cared about Buenos Aires, on the Atlantic. Lima received plentiful supplies of food, livestock, guns, and other Spanish goods. Buenos Aires got the leftovers, or nothing at all.

Buenos Aires lay at the edge of a vast grassy plain known as La Pampa. La Pampa provided rich grazing for herds of horses and cattle. Soon, traders flocked to the settlement to buy and sell swift, beautiful horses. The beef and leather industries flourished too. The people of Buenos Aires discovered that they could do very well without help from the mother country.

Merchants from Buenos Aires wanted the freedom to trade with Great Britain, Portugal, and other European nations. But Spain imposed high taxes, or duties, when Buenos Aires traded with foreign countries. To avoid paying these duties, the porteños became adept at smuggling. As the city grew, its economy was based more and more on illegal trade.

A gaucho on horseback in La Pampa on the outskirts of Buenos Aires

La Pampa (LAH PAHM-PAH)

23

In 1776, Buenos Aires became the capital of a newly created Spanish province called the Viceroyalty of Río de la Plata. The province was ruled by a viceroy appointed by the Spanish Crown. Thirty years later, in 1806, invading British soldiers tested the city's strength. The British conquered Buenos Aires and held it for six weeks before they were driven out. British forces reconquered the city in 1807 but were driven back a second time. Throughout the struggle with the British, the porteños had little help from Spain.

Victory over the British gave the porteños a new sense of confidence. On May 25, 1810, a group of patriots gathered at the Cabildo, or City Council Hall, on the central plaza. They drew up a document

An 1872 illustration of the Plaza del Parque

The British invaded Buenos Aires twice, in 1806 and 1807 (left), but were driven out both times.

An Argentinian plaque depicting a gaucho family on La Pampa

overthrowing the viceroy and appointing their own leader in his place. A British diplomat wrote about the days that followed. "It might have been imagined that endless tumult and disorder would have sprung up, leading directly to pillage and bloodshed. Yet no such disturbances ever took place. All remained quiet. The people have in no instance demanded victims to satisfy their vengeance."

Though Buenos Aires remained fairly calm, Spain did not give up its colony without an armed struggle. Finally, in 1816, the former province became completely independent. From that time forward, it was known as Argentina. Buenos Aires was its capital.

"RICH AS AN ARGENTINE"

At last, the hated duties were abolished. Buenos Aires merchants bought and sold freely with their nation's blessing. Dockworkers loaded ships with great bales of wool, barrels of beef, and bundles of fine leather. Money flowed into the city as though there would never be an end.

Many merchants and their families headed to Europe with their newfound wealth. They bought expensive clothes in London and Paris. Night after night, they attended the opera and the theater. They developed a taste for costly soaps, perfumes, and chocolates. The travelers spent so lavishly that the Europeans developed the saying, "rich as an Argentine."

The Argentines returned home with European ideas about art and culture. They widened downtown streets and planted them with shade trees. They designed elegant houses with pillars and balconies. Buenos Aires merchants even built an opera house to rival the finest halls they had seen abroad.

Not all of the porteños basked in wealth and luxury. Thousands were hungry and wore ragged clothes. Even people with steady factory jobs did not earn enough to support their families. Resentment simmered and rose to a boil. The poor of Buenos Aires waited for a leader who would transform their lives.

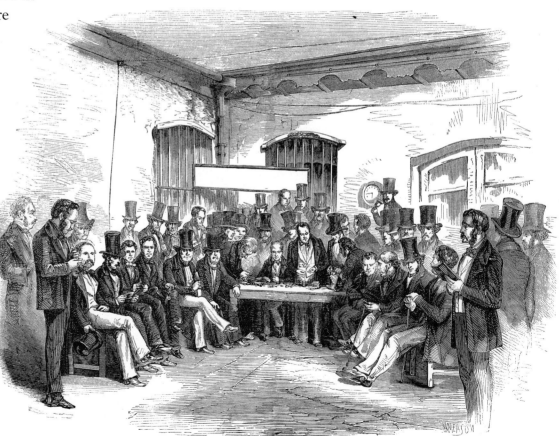

This 1859 illustration shows Buenos Aires merchants conducting business and trade at the Exchange.

Left: The Calle General San Martín (General San Martín Street) as it looked about 1840

Below: Fine leather from Argentina brought high prices in European markets.

THE LADY OF HOPE

One day in 1934, a fifteen-year-old girl named Eva Duarte climbed down from a train at Retiro Station. Like many other poor girls from Argentine villages, she dreamed of becoming a star in the big city. Eva possessed a rare combination of beauty, talent, and poise that helped her to get ahead. Over the years, her voice was often heard on radio soap operas. She appeared in several locally made movies. But she never forgot that she had once been poor, and that millions of others still lived in poverty.

In 1944, Eva Duarte attended a fund-raising party for the victims of a recent earthquake. There she met Juan Domingo Perón, an army colonel with fierce political ambitions. As she explained in her autobiography, Eva stood at his side and declared, "If as you say the cause of the people is your own cause, however great the sacrifice, I will never leave your side until I die."

After Eva Duarte arrived in Buenos Aires, her voice was often heard on radio soap operas.

Eva Duarte (AY-vah DWAR-teh)
Retiro (REH-TEE-roh)
Juan Domingo Perón (HWAHN doe-MEEN-goe peh-RONE)

After his 1950 Loyalty Day speech to workers, President Juan Perón smiles as Eva Perón waves to the crowd from the balcony of Casa Rosada.

Eva married Juan Perón the following year, as he prepared to run for president of Argentina. The working-class people loved her, and called her the "Lady of Hope." She was a great asset in Perón's campaign. Wherever she went, crowds chanted her nickname, "Evita! Evita!"

After Perón was elected, he put Evita in charge of his health, welfare, and labor programs. She opened orphanages, hostels for working girls, and homes for the elderly. The people loved to see her in her dazzling gowns and jewels. Sometimes when she appeared in public, she flung fistfuls of money to her shouting admirers.

An elegantly dressed Eva Perón posed for this picture in 1950.

Eva Perón died of cancer in 1952 at the age of thirty-three. After her death, Perón's popularity crumbled rapidly. Dozens of political scandals came to light, and the people were deeply disillusioned. In 1955, the Argentine military rose up against Perón. The navy bombed the Plaza de Mayo and the Casa Rosada. Perón was overthrown and forced to flee to Spain.

For more than two decades, Argentina reeled under a series of crises. Inflation soared. At times, the price of an ice cream at a Buenos Aires café doubled in the course of a day. Driven by desperation, people broke into stores

Above: A group of jubilant students gathers around a bust of deposed leader Juan Perón. Below: The new military leaders are sworn in.

and stole food that they could not afford to buy. In 1976, a powerful junta, or group of military leaders, seized control of the nation's government. The junta launched a reign of terror that shook the land for the next seven years. Some 10,000 Argentines "disappeared." Into the 1990s, the relatives of these lost men and women called for justice.

In 1983, Argentina established a democratic government at last. Buenos Aires began to revive from its terrible ordeal. Once again, people felt free to talk and laugh on the streets. Once again, they could take pleasure in the delights of their magnificent city.

Recoleta (REH-KOH-LAY-TAH)
Chacarita (CHA-CAH-REE-TAH)
junta (HOON-TAH)

In 1983, after establishing a democratic government, Congress debates a bill reforming the Military Code of Justice.

Till Death Did Them Part

After Evita's death, Perón's enemies seized her embalmed body and took it to Italy. It was not returned to Buenos Aires until the 1970s. Today, Evita lies in a mausoleum in the city's prestigious Recoleta Cemetery. Every year, thousands of people visit her grave as though it were a sacred shrine. Juan Perón, who died in 1974, is buried across town in Chacarita, the cemetery of the common people.

PLAY

Porteños love nothing better than a long, heartfelt discussion. They talk in cafés, taverns, and city parks. Endlessly, they exchange ideas about art, literature, politics, and their own psyches. Buenos Aires has more psychoanalysts than any other city on earth.

But porteños do not spend all their time seeking the answers to serious questions. They also enjoy music, dance, games, and good food. When it comes to having fun, porteños are experts.

THE THUNDER OF HOOFBEATS

Some cities draw thousands of visitors to their sports events. Some are popular sites for business conventions. Still others specialize in opera or ballet. Among the biggest attractions in Buenos Aires are its livestock shows. Each year, 2 million people attend shows sponsored by such organizations as the Rural Agricultural Society and the Argentine Ranchers Association. Open-air corrals and vast, high-ceilinged barns are a sea of stamping, snorting cattle and horses. Eager buyers shout their bids above the din of mooing and neighing.

Livestock shows in Buenos Aires attract millions of people each year.

The noise may not be for everyone—to say nothing of the smell. But these shows display the finest animals La Pampa has produced.

Long ago, La Pampa herds made Buenos Aires a wealthy city. Today, cattle and horses are still essential to the porteño way of life. Porteños consume more beef than the people of any other city in the world. A typical steak is more than 1 inch (2.5 centimeters) thick. Porteño chefs don't let any part of the cow go to waste. They make sausages with beef intestine.

Beef, often in the form of steak (above and right) is the mainstay of the Argentine diet.

Buenos Aires desserts include a wide variety of custards and puddings. An essential ingredient is *dulce de leche*, a kind of thick, sweetened milk. Dulce de leche can be served as a topping on pastries or even spooned up alone for a light snack. Other favorite desserts are *dulce de membrillo* (quince jam) and *dulce de batata con chocolate* (sweet potato with chocolate sauce).

La Pampa has long been known for its exceptional horses. The porteño love of horses and riding is evident at Buenos Aires's two racetracks, the Hipodrómo de San Isidro and the Hipodrómo Argentino. Like racing fans everywhere, porteños add to the excitement by placing bets on the winner. But Buenos Aires fans also have a special appreciation for the grace and beauty of the horses as they surge toward the finish line.

Dulce de leche *is often served as a topping on pastries such as these.*

dulce de leche (DOOL-seh deh LEH-cheh)
dulce de membrillo (DOOL-seh deh memm-BREE-zhoa)
dulce de batata con chocolate (DOOL-seh deh bah-TAH-tah cone choh-coh-LAH-teh)
Hipodrómo de San Isidro (EE-poe-DROH-moe deh sahn eee-SEE-droh)
Hipodrómo Argentino (EE-poe-DROH-moe are-HEN-TEE-noh)

A La Pampa gaucho shows off one of the exceptional horses raised in the region.

A gaucho cattle drive on Estancia Las Palmas

THE ROAR OF THE CROWDS

Polo is one of the most popular sports in Buenos Aires. This polo match is taking place between the Pegasus and Los Indios teams.

Horses are central to the game of polo, one of the most popular sports in Buenos Aires. Polo is played by two mounted teams. Using long-handled wooden mallets, the players try to propel a ball past a goal at the end of the court. Even if you don't understand all the rules, polo is a joy to watch. It is a spectacle of grace and skill, a showcase for highly trained horses and riders.

Like most Latin Americans, porteños are devoted to the game of soccer. Fans pack the stands for contests between neighborhood teams. Rivalries can be fierce. When one team scores a goal, spectators are sometimes swept from their seats in the bleachers by the surging crowds.

The major event for soccer fans comes every four years with the World Cup championship competition. Argentina has consistently produced top-ranking World Cup teams. It won world championships in 1978 and again in 1986, and reached the finals in 1990. Many of Argentina's leading players got their start in the

Soccer, introduced by British sailors in the 1860s, became a national sport in Argentina in 1931.

Wooden mallets like this one are used in the game of polo.

stadiums of La Boca, Núñez, and other Buenos Aires neighborhoods.

Because of the European influence in Buenos Aires, porteños follow some sports that are not popular in other Latin American cities. Professional tennis has many loyal fans. So do the games of cricket and Rugby, the national pastimes of Great Britain.

Cricket somewhat resembles American baseball. In Buenos Aires, cricket matches are held wherever an English community has taken root.

La Boca (LAH BOE-KAH)
Núñez (NOON-YACE)

THE PLEASURES OF MUSIC

When the Colón Theater opened its doors in 1908, Buenos Aires was at the height of its wealth and glory. Modeled on the grand opera houses of Europe, the Colón is a cherished city landmark. Its auditorium is richly decorated in gilt and velvet. It is a splendid backdrop for the National Symphony and the National Ballet of Argentina. The Colón Theater is the world's largest opera house.

For those who cannot afford Colón ticket prices, the symphony plays outdoors in Palermo Park.

The richly decorated Colón Theater (right) is the world's largest opera house.

Figurines that are caricatures of well-known Argentine musicians are popular with collectors.

This gaucho musician is playing several instruments at once.

Buenos Aires offers plenty of other inexpensive entertainment as well. On the weekends, mimes, jugglers, and musicians delight passersby in the parks and along downtown boulevards.

Colón (COH-LONE)
tango canción (TAHN-GO CAHN-SEE-OAN)
Carlos Gardel (CAR-LOCE GAR-DELL)

The Songbird of Buenos Aires

In 1917, the *tango canción*, a tango with poetic lyrics, arose as a musical form in Argentina. A young singer named Carlos Gardel made the tango canción immensely popular. Within a few years, Gardel vaulted to worldwide fame. When he died in a plane crash in 1935, his fans were grief-stricken. Today, his recordings still sell, and fans heap his grave with flowers. People say that Gardel, the Songbird of Buenos Aires, continues to sing better and better every day.

Porteños love all forms of music, from classical to rock. But dearest to their hearts is the tango, their very own musical creation. The tango is a sensual dance played on the violin, guitar, piano, and an accordion-like instrument called the *bandoneón*. Tango songs often have haunting lyrics. They speak of lost love, betrayal, exile, and other heartbreaks. One popular song says:

> Little road that used to be,
> Bordered with clover and flowering rushes,
> Soon you will be a shadow,
> A shadow just like me.

Tango musicians entertain passersby on Caminito Street in the La Boca District of Buenos Aires.

The tango, Argentina's famous national music, originated in Buenos Aires.

The tango arose in the poorest sections of Buenos Aires during the 1880s. At first, the city's upper crust felt the dance and its music were not quite proper. But by the early 1900s, the tango caught on in Europe and the United States. Everyone hummed its lilting tunes. Everyone who was anyone learned its steps.

Today, the tango is still alive and well in Buenos Aires. Devotees crowd into tiny tango clubs that usually don't open their doors until midnight. There, dancers sway to the captivating rhythm, and singers deliver soulful songs of pain, loneliness, and survival.

Tango dancers in La Boca

bandoneón (BAHN-DOH-NEH-OAN)

Argentine writer Jorge Luis Borges loved puzzles and mysteries. Many of his tales involve secret codes and rooms with hidden doors. Borges spent most of his life in Buenos Aires. He said the city was like a labyrinth, full of secret turns and startling surprises. He also found something sure and steady in Buenos Aires. He once described the city as "eternal as air and water."

Jorge Luis Borges (HOAR-HAY LOO-EESS BOAR-HACE)

45

SOUTH OF THE CENTER

Some of the most interesting neighborhoods in Buenos Aires lie south of the historic downtown section. The Cathedral section comes alive at night when its tango clubs open their doors. The neighborhood is named for the Santo Domingo Church, built in 1750. One of the church's chapels proudly displays four banners captured from the invading British in 1806 and 1807. A pair of marble angels guards the tomb of Manuel Belgrano, a hero of the war for independence from Spain.

Above: A sculpture on Caminito Street in the La Boca district
Right: The tomb of Manuel Belgrano, guarded by a pair of marble angels, has a place of honor in Santo Domingo Church.

The neighborhood known as La Boca del Riachuelo was the former harbor for Buenos Aires and the entry point for thousands of immigrants from Italy. Its streets were lined with warehouses and meat-packing plants. Long ago, a visitor described it as a "waste of scattered shanties, dirty and squalid, their wooden boards gaping like rents in tattered clothes." Today, many houses have been repaired and painted in bright colors. La Boca remains one of the most Italian parts of Buenos Aires. The local Spanish is sprinkled with Italian words and phrases, and people line up at their favorite pizzerías. Boca Juniors' Stadium is one of the biggest soccer stadiums in the city.

Colorfully painted houses in La Boca del Riachuelo brighten the neighborhood.

Santo Domingo (SAHN-toe doe-MEEN-goh)
Manuel Belgrano (MON-WELL bell-GRAH-noh)
La Boca del Riachuelo (LAH BOE-kah dell REE-ah-CHWAY-loh)

The San Telmo neighborhood has long attracted artists and writers. The San Telmo Flea Market is held every Sunday at Plaza Dorrego on Calle Defensa (Defensa Street). The flea market is a great place to buy used clothing, almost new kitchenware, and gadgets that might work again someday, given a bit of care and patience.

In 1807, invading British troops marched through the narrow streets of San Telmo. Most of the local men were away at war, but the women put up a fierce resistance. From their roofs and balconies, they poured boiling oil onto the invaders. The British fled for their lives. One of San Telmo's main thoroughfares, Calle Defensa, is named in memory of this event.

Costumed fair goers at the San Telmo Sunday Flea Market

San Telmo (SAHN TELL-MOH)
Plaza Dorrego (PLAH-SAH DOR-RAY-GOH)
Calle Defensa (CAH-ZHEH DEH-FEN-SAH)
Cándido López (CAHN-DEE-DOH LOE-PACE)

Most historians believe that Pedro de Mendoza's original settlement was somewhere in the vicinity of today's Lezama Park. The park is the setting for the National Historical Museum, housed in a magnificent nineteenth-century mansion. The museum's Hall of the Conquest is lined with huge paintings that depict key moments in Spain's conquest of the New World. In one scene, Mendoza and his followers battle with the Querandí Indians. The Hall of Independence displays portraits of Argentine patriots. Outside the museum, visitors can explore the park's winding, tree-shaded paths.

Above: Shopping at the San Telmo Sunday Flea Market
Right: This statue of Pedro de Mendoza, the founder of Buenos Aires, stands in Lezama Park.

The Soldier Painter

One hall in the Historical Museum is dedicated to the splendid murals of Cándido López. In the 1870s, López lost an arm while fighting in a war against the neighboring nation of Paraguay. He went on to become one of Argentina's most renowned painters. His work portrays both the heroism and tragedy of battle.

HEADING NORTH

Recoleta Cemetery is the final resting place of many wealthy Buenos Aires citizens.

Plaza Francia (PLAH-SAH FRAHN-SEE-AH)
Palermo (PAH-LAIR-MOE)
Juan Manuel de Rosas (HWAHN MAHN-WELL DEH ROH-SAHSS)
Justo Jose de Urquiza (HOOSS-TOE HO-SAY DEH OOR-KEY-SEH)

In the 1870s, an epidemic of yellow fever swept Buenos Aires. The wealthiest residents, most of whom lived in San Telmo, fled to the city's northern rim to escape the disease. Many settled in the Recoleta neighborhood. There, they built elegant homes with lush courtyard gardens.

Recoleta hosts wonderful craft fairs at its Plaza Francia (France Square) every Sunday. But the neighborhood is best known for its cemetery. It is the final resting place of the city's elite, who lie in elaborately carved mausoleums. Some say that it is cheaper to live extravagantly all your life than to be buried in Recoleta.

A mother and child (right) are out for a stroll in the Palermo district's beautiful Japanese Botanical Garden (below).

Beyond Recoleta spreads the Palermo neighborhood. Much of this area was once the estate of Juan Manuel de Rosas. Rosas was a ruthless dictator who ruled Argentina from 1829 until 1852. After his death, his estate was given to the people as public parkland. Palermo Park is one of the loveliest parks in Buenos Aires. It contains the city zoo, a polo ground, and an extensive botanical garden. In the park stands a massive equestrian statue of Justo José de Urquiza, the general who brought about Rosas' downfall.

The botanical garden in Palermo Park is a pleasant place to rest and chat.

THE HEART OF THE CITY

Every hour on the hour, deep chimes boom over downtown Buenos Aires. The chimes float from the English Tower, a replica of the famous Big Ben clock in London, England. The square where the tower stands was once called the English Plaza. In 1982, it was renamed the Plaza of the Argentine Air Force.

Broad, tree-lined avenues divide central Buenos Aires into neat, square blocks. High-rise buildings of glass and steel soar above endless rivers of traffic. Here and there, a plaza forms a grassy oasis in the desert of concrete. The Plaza San Martín is named in honor of José de San Martín. A hero of the war for independence, San Martín is regarded as the liberator of Argentina, Chile, and Peru.

The English Tower (Torre de Los Ingleses) *in the Plaza of the Argentine Air Force*

Plaza San Martín (PLAH-SAH SAHN MAR-TEEN)
José de San Martín (HO-SAY DEH SAHN MAR-TEEN)

Left and above: Two views of the Plaza San Martín, in which the equestrian Monument to General José de San Martín (left) holds a place of honor

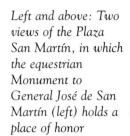

Fighting for the Islands

The world was stunned in April 1982, when Argentina suddenly invaded the British-controlled Falkland Islands. Known to Argentines as the Islas Malvinas, the islands lie about 300 miles (483 km) off Argentina's coast. Argentina's defeat in the Falklands War signaled the downfall of the nation's military government.

Avenida de Mayo
(AH-VEH-NEE-DAH DEH MAH-ZHOA)
Palacio del Congreso (PAH-LAH-SEE-OH DELL CONE-GRACE-OH)
Plaza Congreso (PLAH-SAH CONE-GRACE-OH)
Islas Malvinas (EESS-LAHSS MOLL-VEE-NAHSS)

The Palacio del Congreso (Congressional Palace) stands next to Congress Square, with its elaborate monument to Argentine independence.

The Avenida de Mayo, or May Avenue, runs from east to west through downtown Buenos Aires. At the western end stands the Palacio del Congreso (Congressional Palace), home to Argentina's legislature. With its dome and colonnade, the Palace was modeled on the U.S. Capitol in Washington, D.C. The adjacent Plaza Congreso (Congress Square) is overshadowed by an immense granite monument to Argentine independence. The monument's steep steps represent the Andes Mountains at the nation's western border. The fountain at the monument's base stands for the Atlantic Ocean that laps Argentina's coast.

At the eastern end of the Avenida de Mayo lies the Plaza de Mayo, the symbolic old center of Buenos Aires. The pyramid in the middle of the plaza was built in 1811 to commemorate the first anniversary of Argentina's declaration of independence. Overlooking the square is the Casa Rosada, Argentina's presidential mansion.

Today, the Plaza de Mayo is crowded with people. Most remember the terrible hardships their city has endured. Yet they talk and laugh, looking toward better times ahead. The spirit of hope is alive in the eternal city.

This statue of General Manuel Belgrano (left) stands in the Plaza de Mayo (above).

FAMOUS LANDMARKS

A huge Argentine rabbit on the grounds of the zoo in Palermo Park

The Cabildo, on Plaza de Mayo

The Colón Theater

Plaza de Mayo
Large, grassy park in downtown Buenos Aires. At the center stands a pyramid built in 1811 to commemorate the overthrow of the viceroy in 1810. The plaza is a popular meeting place. Parents bring children on Sundays to feed the pigeons that nest on surrounding rooftops.

National Historical Museum
Extensive museum located in Lezama Park. Exhibits cover Argentina's history from colonial days to the twentieth century.

The Cabildo
The City Council in the days of Spanish rule. In its chambers, patriots signed the 1810 declaration of independence from the Spanish viceroy. Only a small portion of the original building still stands. The Cabildo Museum houses religious art, political documents, and early paintings of the Plaza de Mayo.

Santo Domingo Church
Church completed in 1750. Its Chapel of Our Lady of the Rosary displays four banners captured from the British in 1806 and 1807. One of the church's bell towers still has bullet craters from the war with Britain.

City Museum of Buenos Aires
Museum on the history of the city. Exhibits record how people lived under Spanish rule and during the extravagant era of the late nineteenth century.

Colón Theater
One of the greatest opera houses in the world. Completed in 1908, it is famous for its elegant decor and flawless acoustics. Such greats as Enrico Caruso and Arturo Toscanini have performed here.

Chacarita Cemetery
The cemetery of the common people. President Juan Perón lies here in a small gray stone mausoleum. In 1987, an unknown vandal broke through a skylight and removed the hands from Perón's embalmed body.

The Obelisk that dominates
downtown Buenos Aires

The Plaza de Mayo

Casa Rosada

Recoleta Cemetery
The ornate cemetery of the wealthy of Buenos Aires. Recoleta is the final resting place of Eva Perón. To many of her adoring followers, her tomb is a sacred shrine.

National Museum of Fine Arts
The leading art museum in Buenos Aires. Its collections include works by Monet, Matisse, and other great French impressionists of the late nineteenth century.

The Obelisk
A landmark of downtown Buenos Aires. It is a graceful stone monument standing 220 feet (67 meters) high. It was created in 1936 as part of a national works project to give jobs to the unemployed.

Casa Rosada
The Pink House, or Presidential Palace, overlooking the Plaza de Mayo. The palace was built on the site of an old Spanish fort. In the basement, a museum displays memorabilia of former presidents.

Palermo Park
The largest park in the city. The park contains a zoo, botanical garden, rose garden, livestock fairgrounds, racetrack, polo grounds, and planetarium.

Museum of Hispano-American Art
Art museum in Barrio Norte, north of downtown. Exhibits include wood carvings of saints, paintings, and engraved silver from the colonial era. Plays are performed in the museum's garden.

Penitentiary Museum
One of the most unusual museums in Buenos Aires. Once a women's prison, it displays mementos of prison life in the early twentieth century.

St. Ignatius Church
The oldest church in Buenos Aires. The earliest portions of the building were completed in 1713. A network of tunnels beneath the church may once have been used by smugglers. The tunnels are now open to the public.

FAST FACTS

POPULATION

	1996
Federal District:	3,008,001
Metropolitan Area:	12,500,000

AREA

Federal District:	77 square miles (200 square kilometers)

LOCATION Buenos Aires is located in Argentina on the eastern bank of the Río de la Plata, an estuary of the Atlantic Ocean. The city lies on the edge of the vast grassland known as La Pampa.

CLIMATE Because Buenos Aires lies south of the equator, its seasons are the reverse of those in northern regions. The coldest months are June and July, and the warmest are December and January. The mean temperature in June is 52 degrees Fahrenheit (11° Celsius). In January, the mean temperature is 75 degrees Fahrenheit (24° Celsius). The climate is humid the year round. The heaviest rains occur in March and August.

ECONOMY Buenos Aires is a major international port. Shipping is its most important industry. The metropolitan area also has many factories and meat-packing plants. Manufactured goods include textiles, rubber products, electrical equipment, medicines, and cars.

CHRONOLOGY

1536
Pedro de Mendoza tries unsuccessfully to establish a Spanish settlement at the present-day site of Buenos Aires.

1580
Juan de Garay establishes a permanent Spanish settlement near the site of Mendoza's earlier attempt.

1776
Buenos Aires becomes the capital of the Viceroyalty of the Rió de La Plata, a large Spanish province.

1806
British forces invade Buenos Aires and are driven back after an occupation of six weeks.

1807
The people of Buenos Aires again drive back invading British forces.

1810
Buenos Aires patriots overthrow the ruling viceroy and appoint their own government.

1813
Slavery is abolished in Argentina.

1816
In the northwestern city of Tucumán, Argentina declares its independence from Spain.

1829
Juan Manuel de Rosas takes control of the Argentine government; his bloody rule lasts for more than twenty years.

The gardens on the Plaza de Mayo

1908
The Colón Theater is completed in downtown Buenos Aires.

1946
Juan Perón becomes president of Argentina, claiming to champion the common people.

1955
Perón is overthrown by the Argentine military.

1975
Argentina's military government launches the "Dirty War," imprisoning some 10,000 citizens—the "disappeared ones."

1982
Argentina invades and tries to reclaim the Falkland Islands from the British; the Dirty War comes to an end.

1983
Argentina's military government is overthrown.

1989
Carlos Saúl Menem becomes Argentina's first president of Syrian heritage.

1996
The movie *Evita,* based on the life of Eva Perón, is filmed in Buenos Aires.

BUENOS AIRES

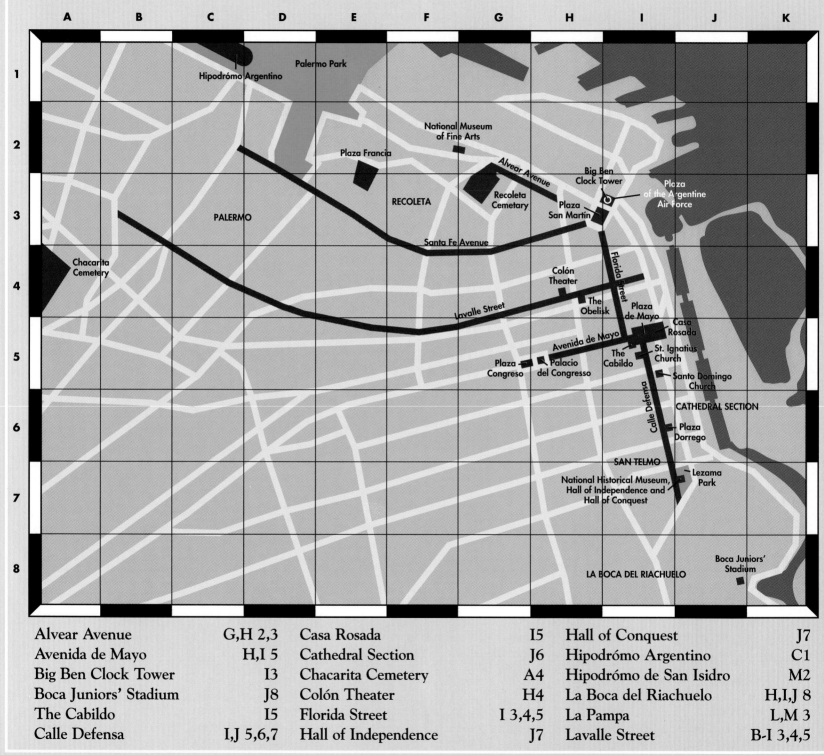

BUENOS AIRES AND SURROUNDINGS

L   M   N   O

1

2

Hipodrómo
de San Isidro

Quintana Avenue   NUÑEZ

3   BUENOS AIRES

Río de la Plata

LA PAMPA

4

GLOSSARY

adept: Expert

boulevard: Broad avenue with a grassy island down the center

colonnade: Decorative series of columns

cuisine: Type of cooking preferred by a particular group or region

dredge: To remove mud in order to make a river more navigable

extravagant: Spending money without concern

labyrinth: Maze

mausoleum: Tomb raised above the ground, usually made of stone

mural: Wall painting

oasis: Refreshing green spot around a spring in a desert

obelisk: Tall, tapered four-sided stone pillar with a pyramid-shaped cap

oppressive: Crushing, cruelly dominating

pillage: Looting and stealing

replica: Exact copy

somber: Grim, gloomy

tumult: Noise and confusion

viceroy: Ruler appointed by a colonial government

Picture Identifications

Cover: Congressional Palace and Monument of the Two Congresses; portrait of two young boys
Title Page: Children playing in a park
Pages 4–5: Obelisk in Plaza de Mayo
Pages 8–9: Boys with skateboards
Pages 20–21: Lezama Park, San Telmo District
Pages 32–33: Costume parade, San Telmo Sunday Fair, Plaza Dorrego
Pages 44–45: Congressional Palace

INDEX

Page numbers in boldface type indicate illustrations

TO FIND OUT MORE

BOOKS

Bernardson, Wayne. *Argentina, Uruguay & Paraguay.* A Lonely Planet Travel Survival Kit. Hawthorn, Australia: Lonely Planet Publications, 1996.

Collier, Simon, et. al. *Tango! The Dance, the Song, the Story.* London: Thames and Hudson, 1995.

Gofen, Ethel. *Argentina.* Cultures of the World series. New York: Marshall Cavendish, 1992.

Greenberg, Arnold and Linda M. Tristan. *Buenos Aires and the Best of Argentina Live Guide.* Edison, N.J.: Hunter Publishing Inc., 1995.

Laffin, John. *Fight for the Falklands!* New York: St. Martin Press, 1982.

Moon, Bernice and Cliff. *Argentina Is My Country.* New York: Marshall Cavendish, 1986.

Otfinoski, Steven. *Argentina Under Juan Peron.* Nations and Their Leaders series. Danbury, Conn.: Franklin Watts, 1998.

ONLINE SITES

Argentina
http://cityguide.lycos.com/southamerica/south_sam/
Links to cities and regions in Argentina, Chile, the Falklands, South Georgia, and the South Sandwich Islands.

Buenos Aires Herald Weekly Online
http://www.buenosairesherald.com/
All the news from the past week, as reported in "Argentina's International Newspaper, Founded in 1876." Argentina and world news, sports, weather, travel tips, and lots more.

Buenos Aires Weather
http://www.intellicast.com/weather/eze
Complete and up-to-date three-day weather forecasts for Buenos Aires, plus plenty of links to other relevant sites.

Fodor's Smart Travel Tips: Buenos Aires
http://www.fodors.com/stt.cgi?dest=Buenos+Aires@11
How far is Buenos Aires from the airport? How much should the taxi ride cost? What's the weather like in January? When are the banks open? How's the water? Here are the answers to these and hundreds of other questions about travel in Buenos Aires.

Postcards from Buenos Aires
http://www.mecon.ar/argentin/bsas/indicei.htm
Click on descriptions to see beautiful full-color images from various places in Buenos Aires.

Southernmost South
http://www.surdelsur.com/historia/indexingles.html
The history of Argentina in words, maps, and pictures.

Virtual Voyager: Argentina
http://www.wp.com/virtualvoyager/argentina.htm
History and information on Argentina and South America: travel tips, links to consulate offices and attractions, plus movies of Buenos Aires and radio broadcasts (if you have the software and the time to download).

World City Guide: Buenos Aires
http://www.world-travel-net.co.uk/cities/bue_hom.htm
Plenty of information about Argentina and Buenos Aires, including a street map of the capital city.

ABOUT THE AUTHOR

Deborah Kent grew up in Little Falls, New Jersey, and received a B.A. in English from Oberlin College. She earned a master's degree from Smith College School for Social Work. After working for four years at the University Settlement House in New York City, she moved to San Miguel de Allende in central Mexico. There, she wrote her first young-adult novel, *Belonging*.